MAP WORKBOOK TO ACCOMPANY
VOLUME II: FROM 1500

WORLD HISTORY

❖•◆•❖

WILLIAM J. DUIKER
PENNSYLVANIA STATE UNIVERSITY

JACKSON J. SPIELVOGEL
PENNSYLVANIA STATE UNIVERSITY

PREPARED BY

CYNTHIA KOSSO
NORTHERN ARIZONA UNIVERSITY

WEST PUBLISHING COMPANY
MINNEAPOLIS/ST. PAUL   NEW YORK   LOS ANGELES   SAN FRANCISCO

WEST'S COMMITMENT TO THE ENVIRONMENT

In 1906, West Publishing Company began recycling materials left over from the production of books. This began a tradition of efficient and responsible use of resources. Today, up to 95% of our legal books and 70% of our college texts and school texts are printed on recycled, acid-free stock. West also recycles nearly 22 million pounds of scrap paper annually—the equivalent of 181,717 trees. Since the 1960s, West has devised ways to capture and recycle waste inks, solvents, oils, and vapors created in the printing process. We also recycle plastics of all kinds, wood, glass, corrugated cardboard, and batteries, and have eliminated the use of Styrofoam book packaging. We at West are proud of the longevity and the scope of our commitment to the environment.

Production, Prepress, Printing and Binding by West Publishing Company.

 TEXT IS PRINTED ON 10% POST CONSUMER RECYCLED PAPER      ∞

ISBN 0–314–03799–3   *

VOLUME TWO
TABLE OF CONTENTS

INTRODUCTION

EXERCISES: CHAPTERS SIXTEEN TO TWENTY-ONE

EXERCISES: CHAPTERS TWENTY-TWO TO THIRTY-THREE

EXTRA MAPS

INTRODUCTION

The creation of maps has a complex and evolving history. It is a very ancient human activity -- the oldest known map, from ca. 5000 BC, was found in central Italy carved on a rock overlooking a Neolithic settlement. Another of the earliest maps still in existence is from the Babylonians in the fifth century BC. In this map the Babylonians are situated precisely in the middle of the universe, all the rest radiated from them -- their own, and particularly the map maker's, perception of the world. As the Babylonian map shows, human viewpoint as an element in map making is inevitable.[1]

Maps tell us about the physical and cultural aspects of the world, but they can be deceiving. Every map has a point of view or perspective. It has an author (the cartographer), a subject, and a theme. The subject and theme represent the author's interest, but also his or her skills, knowledge of geography, political viewpoints, and historical context. All map makers, therefore, pick a perspective from which to display their particular purpose or orientation, which occasionally is an intentionally false one. Colors, for example, can be and have been used to suggest subtly "good guys" or "bad guys." Countries can be drawn smaller or larger to suggest relative importance. To confuse an "enemy," the map maker may include incorrect details. A world map from the 16th century will show the continents as far as they were known to the Europeans during this age of discovery, but not as we believe them to be today. Any later chart of the Americas will depict the continent as very different in size and shape (clearly, the continents themselves did not change that much). Again, the world map reveals many things about the authors. The interest and knowledge of the author is further revealed by the selection of details for the map. In even the most "objective" map, however, one simply cannot add all details in all maps. The map would be rendered incomprehensibly complicated. Thus, maps do not represent reality, but a version of reality. Maps are like snapshots of the world, a moment in time and space with a definite historical context.

Despite this, there are several basic principles governing the structure and reading of maps, and map reading remains an important part of any person's basic knowledge about the world, whether for travel or keeping track of events around the world. When someone gives you directions, or asks them of you, your brain automatically attempts to

---

[1] I would like to thank the undergraduate students, and in particular Clyde Wilson, in the History of Western Civilization courses at Northern Arizona University. They provided indispensable help and advice in the development of this workbook.

draw a rudimentary map. Your mind may even see roads as lines and rivers as bands or buildings as small squares.

To understand the basic appearance of a map, imagine the world as you see it from an airplane. The very straight lines that you see are generally roads and highways. The winding bands are rivers. Rectangles may be buildings and large dark green masses are forests. Cities are conglomerations of rectangles. If you simply took a picture from your airplane and had it printed you would have a photographic map: a reduced representation of a portion of the surface of the earth.

How we see the world from an airplane is, however, somewhat different from how we see it on a map. The world is round. The map page is flat. All map makers, therefore, pick a perspective (as we have seen) and a scale from which to display their particular purpose or orientation.

Finding the exact location of any place requires several steps. To make matters more difficult, reproducing a location accurately is complicated by the fact noted above: the world is round and most maps are not. This fact of life leads to unavoidable distortion is the spatial representation of locations. (You may notice that the shapes of continents change slightly from map to map. This is because the distortion is different depending upon the perspective of the map.) Flat maps, however, are not likely to be completely superseded by globes. Carrying a globe on a hike or road trip would be very inconvenient.

In order to make a map (or to read one) a frame of reference is chosen. A grid system within the frame of reference is usually used to help pinpoint locations on the map. In this exercise book, the grid pattern has been removed in order to make the maps less cluttered, but normally the lines of latitude and longitude would be included on the map. These lines appear on most of the maps in your text.

Map makers, in order to build a grid system, chose the north and south poles as two definite, and not arbitrary, points from which to begin dividing the world. Midway between these poles a line was drawn around the world (this is the equator). The lines of latitude run parallel to the equator up and down to each pole. The equator provides a natural line from which to measure, but there is no such natural longitude line (but one is put in by convention and is called the prime meridian). A longitudinal starting point is obviously needed as a point of reference. Lines of longitude complete the grid by drawing lines from pole to pole around the planet (the standard one passing through Greenwich, England for historical reasons -- now the commonly accepted prime meridian).

The longitudinal line through Greenwich, England is now used as an accepted reference point, but many nations have, in the past, created maps with their own most important cities as reference points. The United States made maps with Washington DC as the prime meridian. Spain drew it through Madrid, the Greeks through Athens, the Dutch through Amsterdam and so on.

Many different scales of maps are also used. That simply means that there are maps with different proportions between the distance on the map and the actual distance on the world. The larger the fraction (or proportion), the smaller the territory covered. Inches per mile or centimeters per kilometer are the most common kind of scale. The scale is merely a fraction comparing the distances on the map measured in inches or centimeters, with the distances on the ground measured in miles or kilometers (e.g., 1 inch on the map = 10 miles on the ground).

Although the entire process insures that maps will always represent a <u>version</u> of reality, instead of reality itself, maps are becoming more and more accurate.[2] Cartographers have worked to produce perfect maps since the late middle ages, with much success. This success is our gain, as it enhances our understanding of history, geography, meteorology, cultural and economic distributions of people, ... the list is endless.

That is precisely the purpose of this exercise book -- to help you learn to read and understand maps as well as to help you understand the relation between places and people through time. The maps will help you order events and historical locations. Nearly all exercises incorporate three parts. There is a brief introduction to each exercise. The section marked "locations" asks you to find and correctly place on the map provided cities, boundaries and other features. The "questions" section asks you to attempt to relate, or synthesize, the historical and geographical information that you have absorbed.

BRIEF BIBLIOGRAPHY

Demko, George with Jerome Agel and Eugene Boe. 1992. *Why in the World, Adventures in Geography*. New York: Doubleday. This is a fun and easy to read introduction to mapping and geography. It does an excellent job of pointing out the importance of geography.

Greenhood, David. 1964. *Mapping*. Chicago: University of Chicago Press. This book provides a clear and concise introduction to maps and mapping.

Wood, Denis. 1992. *The Power of Maps*. New York: The Guilford Press. In this book Wood shows how maps are used and abused. It is an excellent introduction to the way maps have been used by groups and individuals to make an argument or present a point of view.

---

[2]The new, 1993, <u>Hammond, Atlas of the World</u>, is a beautiful example of this trend.

2

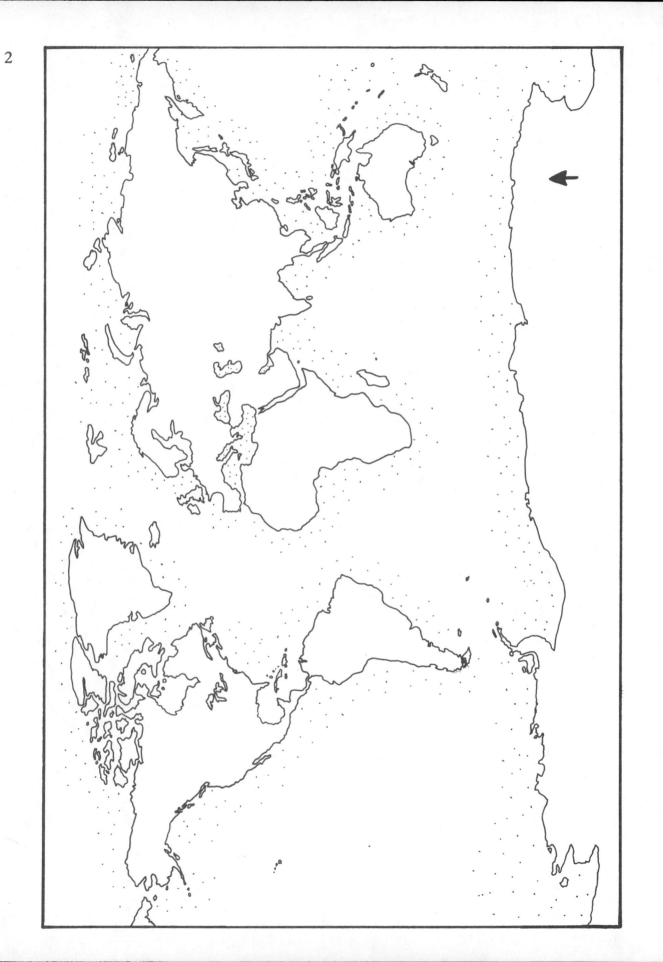

Exercise 1
The World: Major Regions

(Maps: use an atlas of your choice)

Introduction

This exercise puts into perspective the major regions of the planet, as we know them today. Civilizations developed and transformed themselves in a world context. They were not, and are not, isolated entities. Interactions among the various regions and people are evident from very early in human history. People traded, and continue to trade, with one another for food, tools and raw materials. In that process, they learned about one another, sometimes adopting practices, sometimes improving upon the technologies and customs that they found.

Locations

With different colored marking pens or pencils, shade or draw in and label the following regions and geographical features. You may number the locations and place the numbers on the map for clarity.

1. Regions: Egypt, Fertile Crescent, Anatolia, Iberian Peninsula, Balkan Peninsula, North Africa, Britain, Iran, Russia, China, North America, Arabia, South America, Southeast Asia, Japan, Australia

2. Rivers: Tigris, Nile, Danube, Rhine, Mississippi, Ganges, Amazon, Yangtze

3. Seas, Oceans, Lakes: Mediterranean, Black Sea, Persian Gulf, Red Sea, Atlantic Ocean, North Sea, Indian Ocean, Pacific Ocean, Caribbean, Great Lakes

4. Mountains: Caucasus, Alps, Apennines, Taurus, Pyrennes, Rockies, Himalayan Mts.

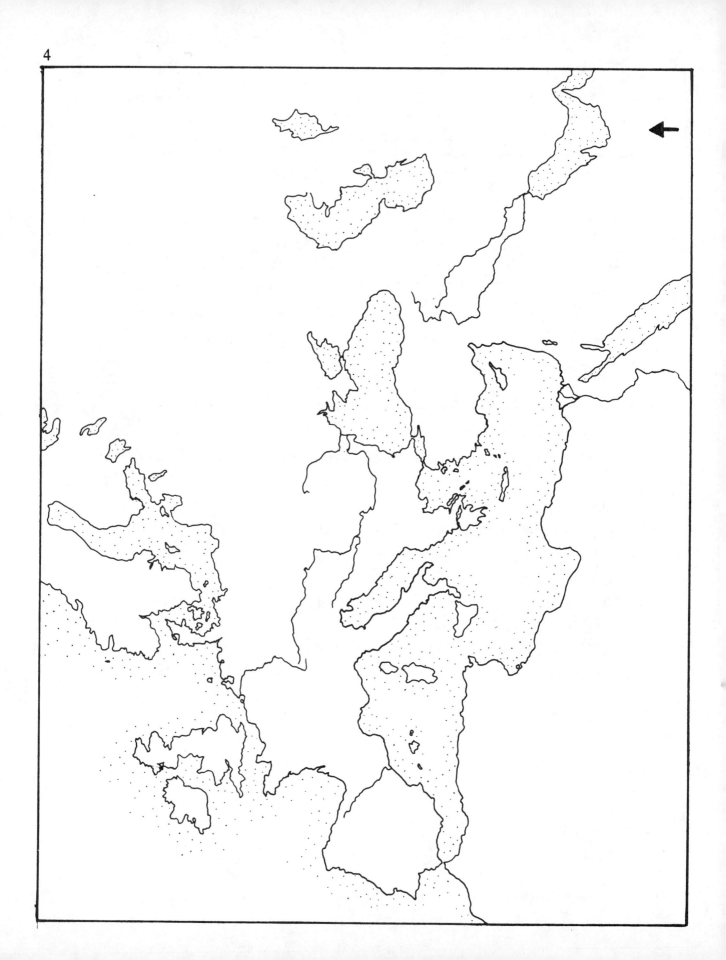

Exercise 2
Catholics and Protestants: 1550 AD

(Map 16.1)

Introduction

In the sixteenth century abuses by the Catholic church, in particular the Papacy, were reaching a crisis point. Many reform movements grew out of the frustration of the times, some made surprisingly influential by the dissemination of these new ideas through the written word, now easily spread because of the printing press. The reformation in Germany was to be one of the most influential. This particular reform movement was led by Martin Luther, the founder of Lutheranism. It was not long before the population of Europe had chosen sides: Protestant (e.g. Lutheran, Calvinist, Anglican) or Catholic. This exercise identifies some of the divisions, by religion, that appeared by the mid sixteenth century.

Locations

On your map, label the following cites and countries. Next to each label write in the local religion (e.g. Dijon-Roman Catholic).

1 . Cities: London, Dublin, Edinburgh, Munich, Paris, Lisbon, Seville, Rome, Trent

2 . Countries: Norway, Sweden, Denmark

Questions

Compare and contrast the Reformation in England and Germany. Were the same reforming factors at work? Who initiated the Reformation in England? In Germany?

What impact did the Reformation have on society in Europe? Give several examples.

Exercise 3
European Conquests and Possessions in the West Indies

(Maps 17.1, 17.2)

Introduction

In 1492 a new era in world history was launched. European adventurers took their ships in search of wealth, fame and new worlds to conquer and convert. These men provoked a transformation of Africa, Asia, the America's and Europe itself. This exercise looks at just one small part of the world affected by the European voyages and conquests.

Locations

With different colored marking pens or pencils, shade in and label the following islands or regions and European spheres of influence

1. Islands or regions: Cuba, Puerto Rico, Lesser Antilles, Jamaica, Belize, Mosquito Coast, Florida, Bahamas

2. Spheres of influence: lightly shade in the Spanish and English areas of interest and control

Questions

What motivated European settlement in the West Indies? Discuss the short and long term impact of European settlement on the people and environment of the West Indies. What impact did the discovery of the West Indies have on the countries and people of Europe?

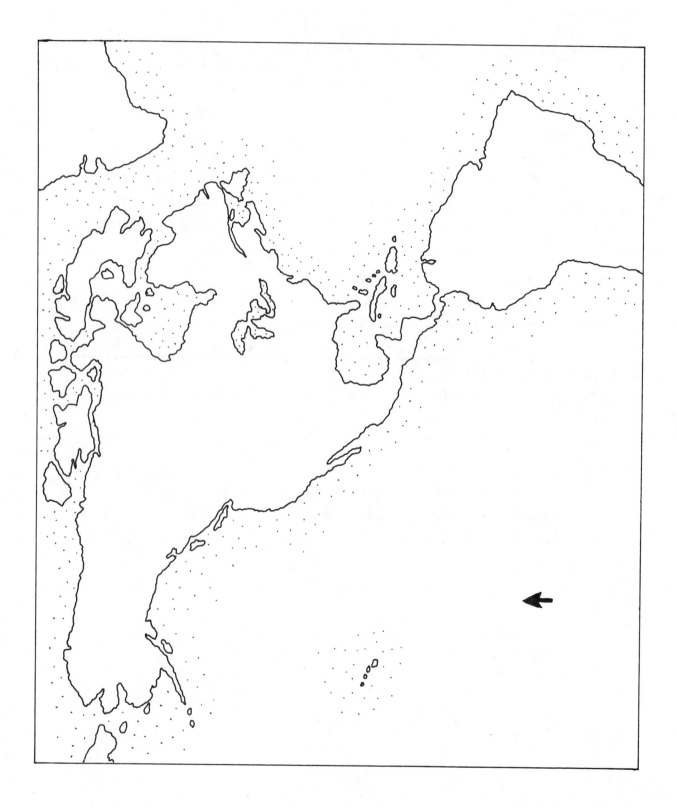

Exercise 4
Colonization and Independence in North America

(Maps 17.1, 17.2, 17.3, 21.2, 21.4, 22.6)

Introduction

With the discovery of the Americas by the Europeans, a new era was begun. European powers claimed these territories for themselves, regardless of the original inhabitant's desires. Europeans brought with them a new way of life and old conflicts. It took hundreds of years to sort out these conflicts fought on American soil.

This exercise introduces you to the European territories of North America.

Locations

A. On the map provided lightly shade in, using different colors, the following areas of European influences, control and colonies (by the 18th century): Spanish, French, English, and Dutch

B. Now mark the boundary of the territory of the USA in 1803 and in 1848. Also mark the boundary of the territory of Canada in 1867 and in 1912.

C. Place the following cities on your map: Boston, Winnipeg, New York, New Orleans, Philadelphia, Chicago, Quebec, Vancouver, Washington DC, San Francisco and Denver.

D. Place or label the following geographical features on your map: Missouri River, Mississippi River, Colorado River, The Great Lakes, Hudson Bay.

Questions

In general, what happened to the societies found in North America by the European powers? What explains European military successes over these societies?

By what means and for what reasons did the new USA free itself from British rule? How was this move similar and different from developments in Canada?

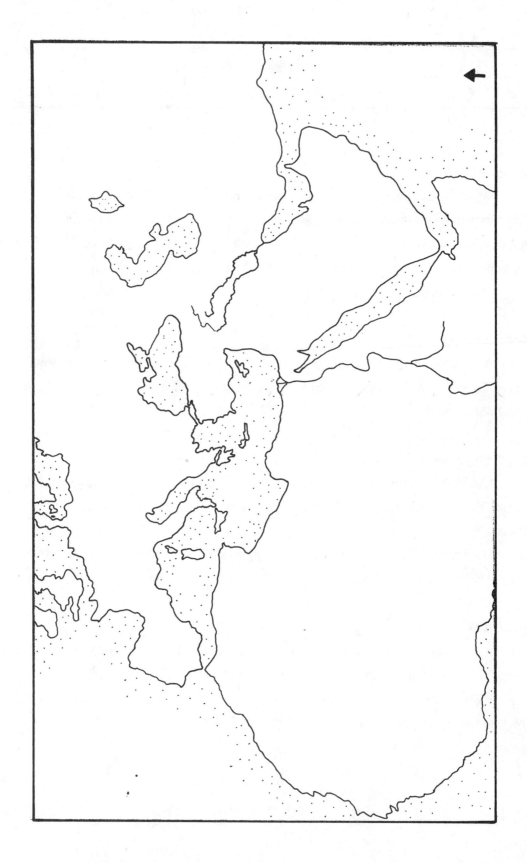

Exercise 5
The Turks and Their Neighbors

(Maps 18.1, 18.2, 18.3)

Introduction

Muslim empires dominated the Middle East and South Asia for several centuries. Despite European pressure, they brought stability to a traditionally unsettled region until the eighteenth century. By the end of the eighteenth century the powerful Ottoman Empire of the Turks had gradually begun to decline in power.

This exercise introduces you to the Middle East.

Locations

With different colored marking pens or pencils, label the following cities, people, regions and geographical features and shade in the following imperial boundaries

1. Cities: Damascus, Istanbul, Aleppo, Salonica, Isfahan, Tabriz

2. People: Uzbeks, Circassians

3. Regions and geographical features: Crimea, Georgia, Najd, Morea, Mediterranean Sea, Persian Gulf, Caspian Sea, Aral Sea, Euphrates River, Black Sea

4. Boundaries: Ottoman and Safavid empires at their height; also draw in the western boundary of the Mughal Empire

Questions

What factors allowed the Ottomans to overthrow the Byzantine Empire in the 15th century? What factors finally limited the expansion of the Ottoman Empire into the Balkans? What are the main differences and similarities among the Moslem empires discussed in chapter 18?

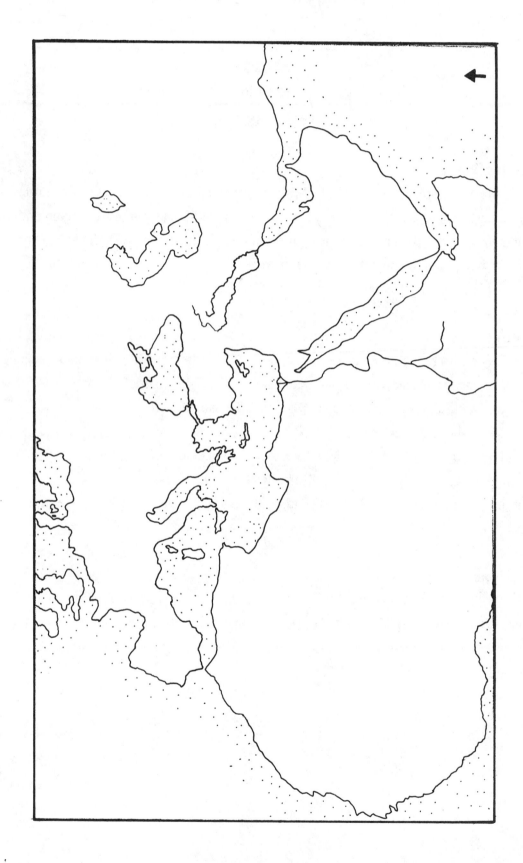

Exercise 6
The Ottoman Empire

(Maps 18.1, 18.2)

Introduction

The Turkish people, led by the Ottomans, conquered the Byzantine Empire once and for all in 1453 with the capture of Constantinople. This was a tremendous victory and afterwards the Turks were on the move. They added vast tracts of lands to their wealthy empire.

The Ottomans were very effective at getting the Europeans to accept them as an equal power. They had a very intricate and effective government, with a strong and well organized military. This exercise traces the growth of Ottoman strength and influence in Europe and the Mediterranean regions.

Locations

With different colored marking pens or pencils trace the boundaries of the Ottoman empire at 1451, at 1481, 1521 and 1566. Also label the following regions and cities.

1. Cities: Cairo, Damascus, Istanbul, Athens, Belgrade, Tunis
2. Regions: Syria, Egypt, Wallachia, Moldavia, Transylvania, Anatolia

Questions

After 1566 the northern boundaries of the Ottoman empire were fairly fixed. What occurred to stop further movement in that direction? What were the strengths and weaknesses of the Ottomans? What were the long term results of their conquests?

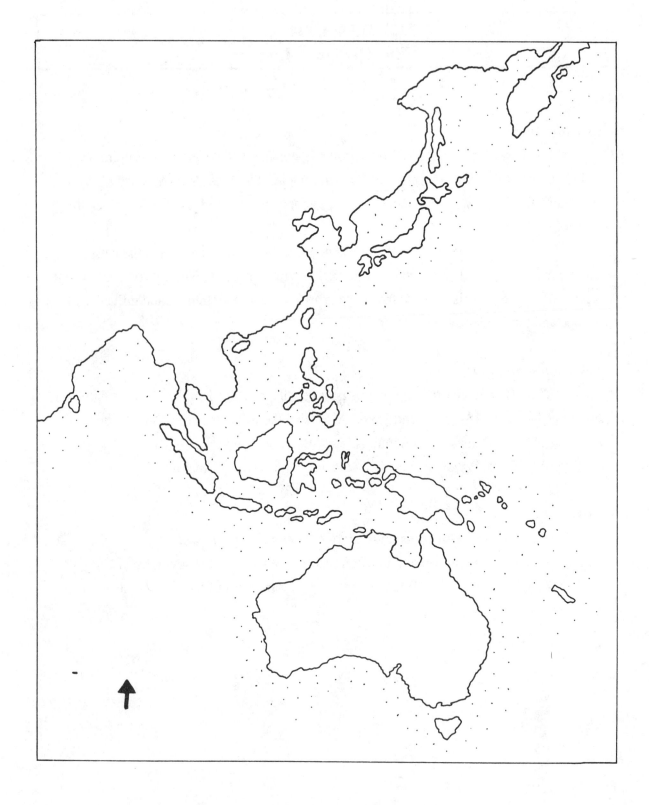

Exercise 7
East Asia: 1500-1800

(Maps 19.1, 19.2)

Introduction

Vital new societies continued to develop in East Asia. Chinese and Japanese cultures earned the admiration and envy of neighbors and European observers. When the Portuguese first encountered the Chinese, this eastern civilization was the most advanced on earth.

In Japan, the 15th century ushered in an era of rivalries, but by the mid-16th century a process of unification had begun. Once in power, the dominant Tokugawa rulers initiated a long period of peace. This allowed economic growth and the flowering of Japanese cultural arts, such as literature, drama, pottery and painting.

Locations

A. Draw in the boundary of the Qing empire

B. With different colored marking pens or pencils, label the following cities, regions and states.

1. Cities: Changsha, Canton, Nanjing, Beijing, Wuhan, Tsugaru, Sakai, Todo, Asano, Kuroda, Hosokawa

2. Regions and states: Hunan, Vietnam, Taiwan, Cambodia, Yunnan, Manchuria, Inner Mongolia, Shadong, Sichuan, Burma, Guandong

Questions

Describe the factors that led to the decline and fall of the Ming dynasty. Who were the Qing and how did they consolidate their power? Using map 19.2, list the states that participated in the tributary system of the Qing. What factors led to their incorporation into the system? Were they willing or unwilling participants?

What motivated the Japanese to isolate themselves from western cultures? Were they able to succeed?

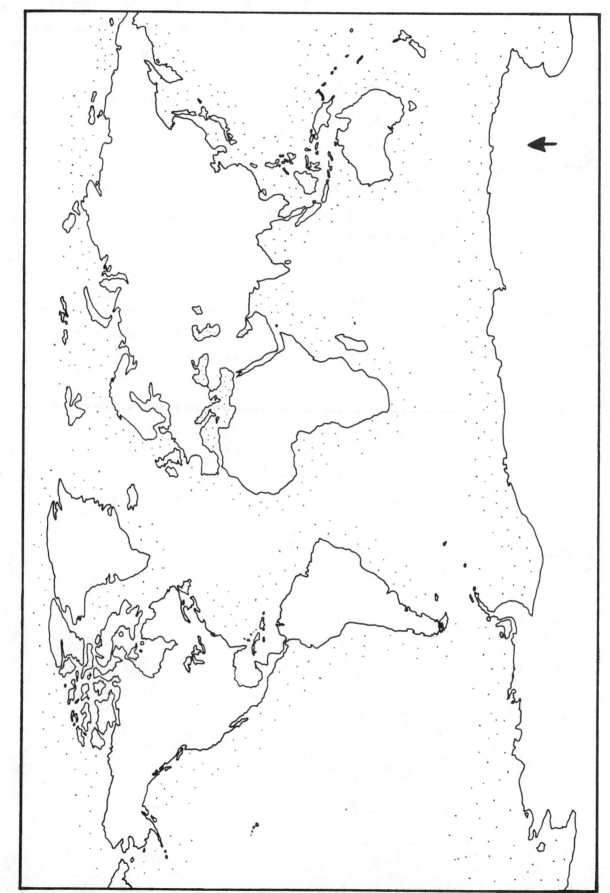

Exercise 8
Development of World Empires: 1783-1914

(Maps 21.3, 21.4, 21.5, 21.6, 24.1, 24.2, 25.3)

Introduction

The European states of the eighteenth and early nineteenth centuries were characterized by growth and rivalries. Unfortunately for the rest of the world, these rivalries were not all played out at home. The main powers became very interested in the concept of a balance of power. This meant they felt the need to limit the power of some states and expand and support the power of others, both near and far. The tools used for this process were mainly two: diplomacy and the military. Foreign ministries sprouted in far off places and the sizes of standing armies were increased. Maritime powers increased the sizes of their navies.

Countries which were not at the same level of industrial development were claimed for their natural resources and people by the European powers. This exercise looks at the European territories of this era, as well as some of the uses and abuses put to them.

Locations

A. On the world map provided, lightly shade in different colors, the spheres of influence and territories of the following empires: Spanish, Portuguese, British, Dutch, Ottoman, Russian, French.

B. Trade in many kinds of goods flourished in the growing international economy. The colonies produced agricultural goods in increasing demand in Europe (coffee, sugar, cotton and tobacco especially) and in these colonies slave worked plantation economies developed. Thus the most notorious of trade "goods" were in great demand: the people from Africa. Next, trace the main routes of the slave trade to the colonies.

Questions

What territories were exploited for the slave trade? What were the main destinations of these Africans? Be explicit. What were the eighteenth century arguments for and against slavery?

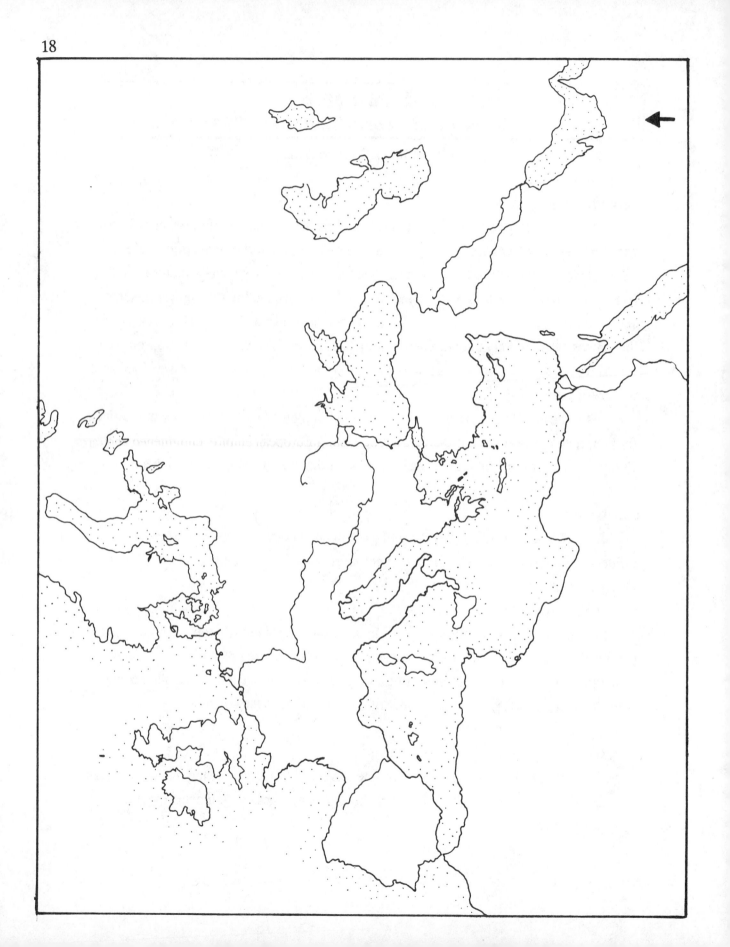

Exercise 9
Napoleon's Empire

(Maps 21.5, 21.6)

Introduction

The late eighteenth century saw two important revolutions in the west: the American revolution and the French revolution. Both were the result of long term problems. The French sought, like the Americans, to ground their constitution in the idea of equal rights. The implementation of equal rights was neither easy nor peaceful. Other European nations feared that violent upheaval would spread from France and, thus, an informal coalition formed against the French. In response, the French had built up a large and impressive army and conquered even the Netherlands.

Terror, instability and confusion soon dominated French politics and the economy. This situation allowed Napoleon to stage the coup d'état that would bring him to power. With his power he would try to create a long-lasting European empire, enlightened and fair. This exercise traces the growth of the Napoleonic state in Europe.

Locations

With different colored marking pens or pencils outline the boundaries of the French Republic and its satellites. Label the satellites. Next mark the boundaries of the French Empire under Napoleon as well as those territories under French control.

Questions

What lands were gained by Napoleon? His was not a long lived empire. Why not? What factors ultimately led to his downfall?

Generally what were the results of the revolutions of the eighteenth century? What were some of the major social, political, and territorial changes?

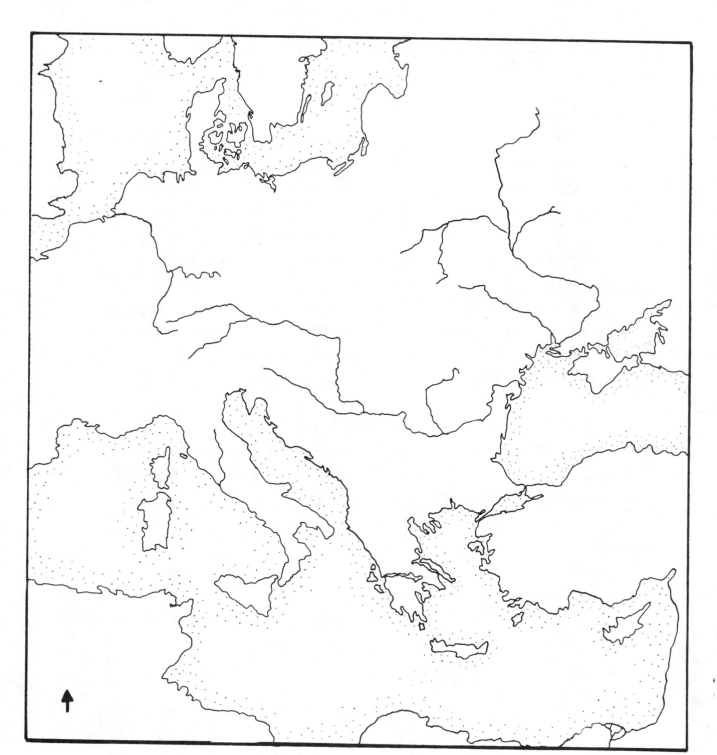

Exercise 10
The German States in the Eighteenth Century

(Maps 21.5, 21.6)

Introduction

After the end of the Thirty-Years war, Germany was still made up of more than three hundred independent states. The Holy Roman Empire was an entity in name only. Out of the hundreds of German states, two became most powerful: Brandenburg and Austria. Both of these states would grow and strengthen because of particularly dominating families, the Hohenzollerns and the Hapsburgs respectively.

The boundaries and peoples of these regions of Europe were mobile and unstable. This exercise is intended to give you an idea for how these German and Slavic regions were defined.

Locations

With a marking pen or pencil label, date, and draw the boundaries (with as much accuracy as possible) for the following Germanic, Austrian and Slavic states and regions. Also label the following cities.

1. States: Prussia, Poland, Austria, Hungary, Bulgaria, Ukraine, Bosnia, Serbia, Russian Empire

2. Regions: Bavaria, Crimea, Prussia, Saxony

3. Cities: Dresden, Vienna, Cracow, Budapest, Venice, Prague, Breslau, Nuremberg, Warsaw, Munich

Questions

What were the long term goals of the Hohenzollern dynasty? How successful were they in achieving their goals?

The Austrians had long been important. Describe the Austrian government. What factors made it develop as it did? Why did the Hapsburgs decide to move into more eastern territories and abandon the thought of a purely German empire?

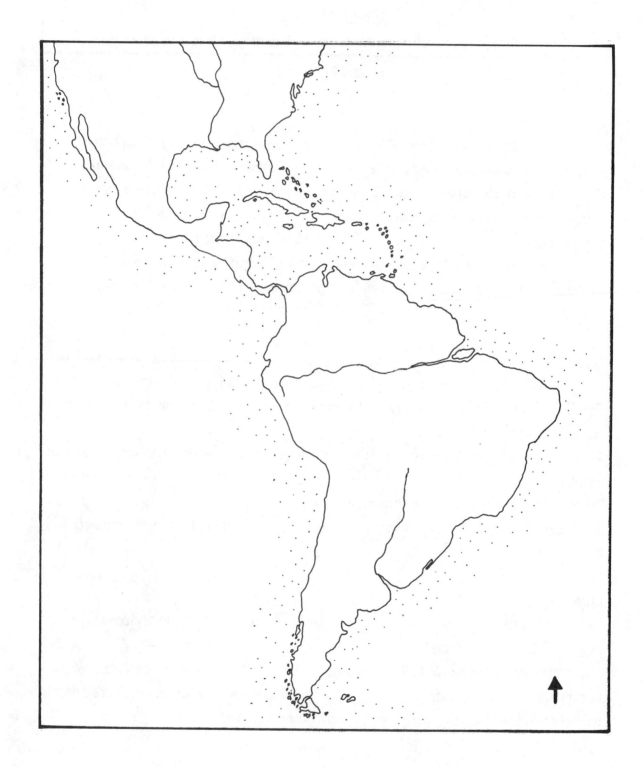

Exercise 11
Colonization and Independence in Central and South America

(Maps 21.3, 22.3, 29.3)

Introduction

Latin America holds a special fascination for those of us residing in North America. In politics the United States has felt the area to be of vital National interest and has thereby justified centuries of interference in the internal workings of national states. Yet despite this continual contact, as a people, we North Americans have lacked understanding of our southern neighbors, with their Spanish and Native influences.

This exercise introduces you to the regions of Central and South America and shows you how recently some of these states have achieved independence.

Locations

With different colored marking pens or pencils trace the boundaries of the and label the following colonies, cities, and independent states.

1. Colonies: Shade in the areas colonized by the French, Portuguese, Spanish, English and Dutch

2. Cities: Locate the following on your map Santa Fe, Caracas, Rio de Janeiro, Lima, Bogotá, Quito and Sao Paulo

3. Independent states: Draw in the borders and label with name and date of independence the following: Haiti, Dominican Republic, Nicaragua, Colombia, Costa Rica, Peru, Brazil, Chile, Argentina, Bolivia, Ecuador,

Questions

Which states most recently achieved independence? Which regions resisted colonization the longest, and why? What factors led to and encouraged the growth of the independence movement?

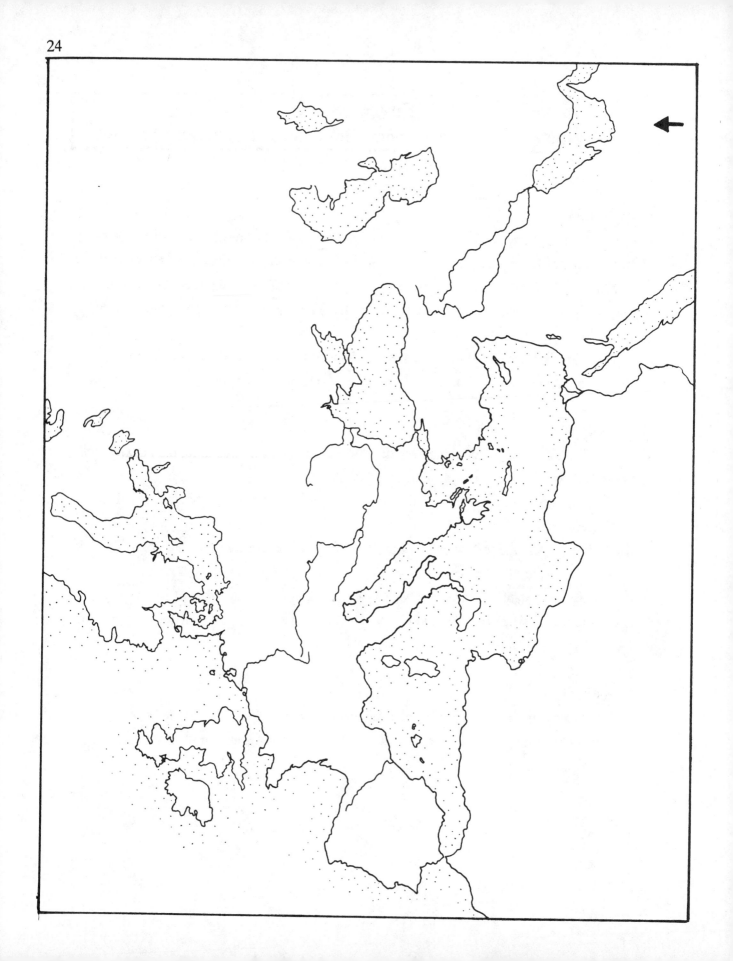

Exercise 12
Europe in 1815

(Map 22.1)

Introduction

By 1815 a measure of territorial stability was restored to the European continent. In some case the old monarchies were also restored. Peace arrangements were made in an attempt to contain the forces for change unleashed in the late eighteenth century. Such attempts would prove to be futile in the long run. This exercise provides a familiarity with the nations of the early nineteenth century.

Locations

With colored marking pens or pencils label and draw the boundaries the following nations: Spain, Portugal, France, Great Britain, Netherlands, Switzerland, the Papal States, Kingdom of the Two Sicilies, Denmark

Questions

Briefly describe the problems that the conservative movement had in containing the forces for change. What role did Metternich play in these conservative attempts to maintain order? Name three areas where there were revolts and describe the European response.

Exercise 13
Independent Nations of Latin America (1845)
(Map 22.2)

Introduction

The revolutions that freed North America had little immediate effect on the colonial status of countries in South and Central America. These lands remained in the hands of colonial powers into the nineteenth century. The Spanish and the Portuguese held these territories and were loath to give up their wealth, even though their powers were weakening. Slowly the lands of South America demanded and got independence, despite Spanish use of well trained troops to quell the rebellions.

Locations

With a marking pen or pencil label, draw the boundaries and provide the date of independence for the following nations of South and Central America: Ecuador, Columbia, Brazil, Peru, Bolivia, Paraguay, Uruguay, Chile, Argentina, Venezuela, Guatemala, El Salvador, Honduras, Nicaragua, Costa Rica

Questions

Which Latin American states failed to gain their independence at this time (1845)? What role did the United States play in movement for independence in Latin America? Why did the United States become involved?

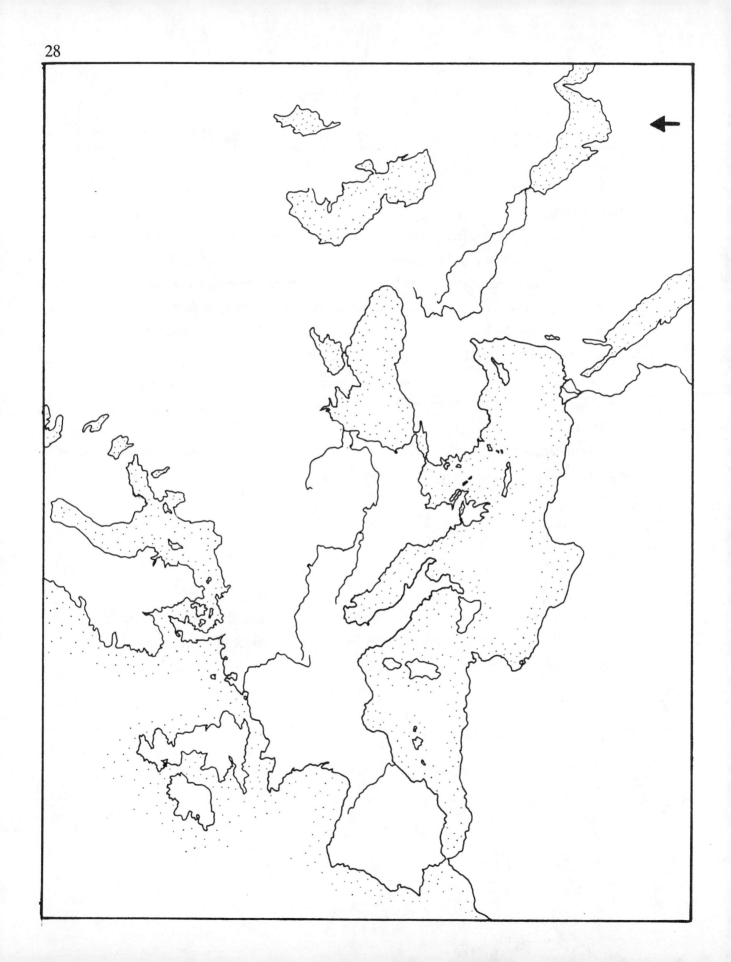

Exercise 14
Revolution and Unification: Europe in 1871

(Maps 22.4, 22.5, 23.1, 23.2, 23.4)

Introduction

Despite the attempts to keep the lid on change, a new wave of revolution and reform spread across Europe in the second half of the nineteenth century. Again the French took a leading role. The 1830's to the 1850's saw revolts in Spain, Portugal, France, Italy, Russia and Poland. By the 1870's the map of Europe had again changed.

Locations

On the map provided draw the boundaries of and label the following European states and regions as of 1871.

1. States: Spain, France, Belgium, Great Britain, German empire, Austria-Hungary, Switzerland, Greece, Ottoman Empire, Denmark, Italy

2. Regions: Croatia-Slovenia, Bosnia, Albania, Serbia

Questions

Compare map 22.1 to the map that you have just completed. What are the major differences between the two? What states have been eliminated, made smaller or enlarged? Briefly explain the process by which Italy and Germany became unified. What main factors allowed them to unify?

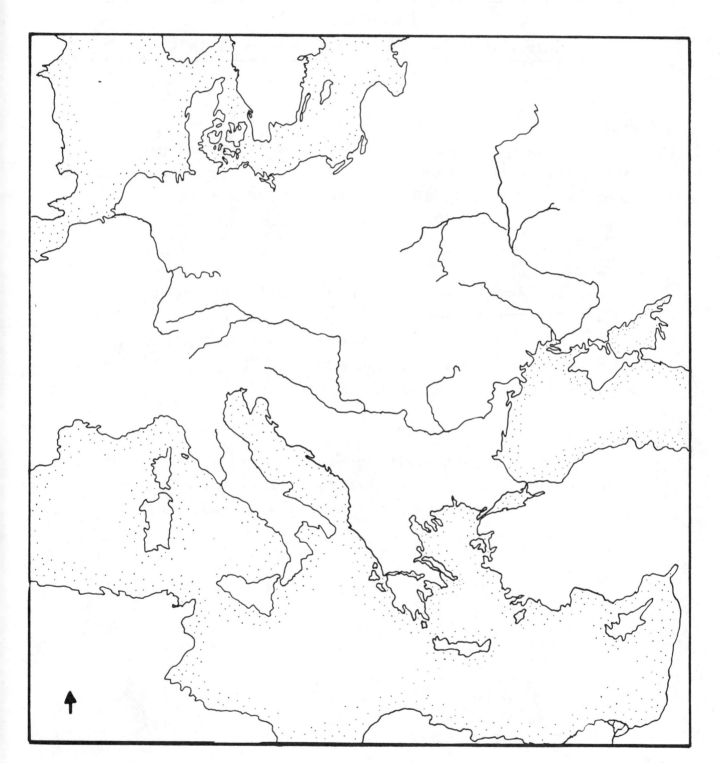

Exercise 15
The Balkans: 1878-1913

(Maps 23.2, 23.3)

Introduction

Crises in the Balkans have commonly occurred over the centuries. In 1908 the Balkan states of Bosnia and Herzegovina were annexed by Austria. The Serbs, because their hopes for a larger Serbian kingdom were dashed, responded by precipitating an international incident. In 1912 more attention was drawn to the region when the Ottoman Turks were defeated in the First Balkan war. New divisions of territories resulted. 1913 saw another war and further divisions of the Balkans. This exercise traces these divisions of the Balkans prior to World War I.

Locations

A. With different colored marking pens or pencils outline the boundaries of the Balkan states after the Congress of Berlin in 1878. Label Serbia, Macedonia and Greece.

B. Next trace the boundaries of the Balkan states as of 1913. Label Serbia, Montenegro, Albania, Greece, Bulgaria, Rumania and Austria-Hungary

Questions

What happened to Macedonia? What happened to the Ottoman possessions in the Balkans? And under whose control were the Bosnians and Herzegovinians?

What were the goals and motivations of the Serbians in the Balkan wars? Were they successful in reaching their goals? What were the long-term results of the Balkan Wars?

Exercise 16
India: 17th - 20th Centuries

(Maps 18.4, 24.4, 30.2, 31.1)

Introduction

India, like other Asian countries, was exploited by western powers for centuries. Colonial policies would eventually give rise to strong nationalistic movements, which were able to overthrow the colonial powers. The British were expelled from India in the 20th century. This exercise looks at the peninsula of India.

Locations

A. On the map provided shade in and label the following geographical features, regions and cities

1. Geographical features: Arabian Sea, Bay of Bengal, Indian Ocean, Indus River, Ganges River

2. Regions: Ceylon, Mysor, Bengal, Kashmir, Marathas, Punjab, Burma, Assam

3. Cities: Bombay, Delhi, Lahor, Calcutta, Benares, Hyderabad, Bangalore, Bhopal, Simla

B. Draw a boundary around India under British control in the 19th century.

C. Shade in the areas that became Bangladesh and Pakistan in the 20th century. Mark the areas that are being disputed between China and India.

Questions

How did India win its independence form the British? Why did it then split into several independent nations? Try to explain why China and India still have boundary disputes.

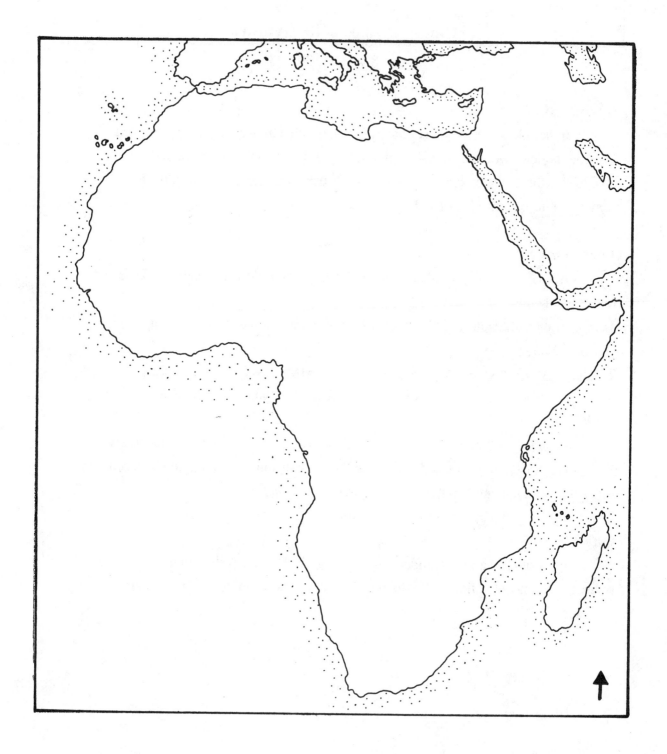

Exercise 17
Africa: European Control in 1914

(Map 25.2)

Introduction

In the latter years of the nineteenth century European states were again interested in overseas expansion. The Americas were lost to them so they renewed their attentions toward Asia and Africa. They were not, however, able to dominate the territories in Asia and Africa quite like they had done in earlier centuries. Still, these new colonies were worth the trouble as they provided many benefits, both material and social.

Locations

Africa was carved up among the Europeans, with only Ethiopia and Liberia as independent nations. With different colored marking pens or pencils, color in and identify (for example, make all French territory blue and provide a legend) the territory claimed by France, Germany, Italy, Great Britain, Belgium, Portugal and the Boer Republic. Label Ethiopia, Congo, Algeria, Egypt, Kenya, Madagascar and Angola.

Questions

What were the benefits (economic, social, political) of African colonies to the Europeans? Briefly, what were some of the effects of this colonialism on the continent of Africa? Why were Liberia and Ethiopia able to remain independent?

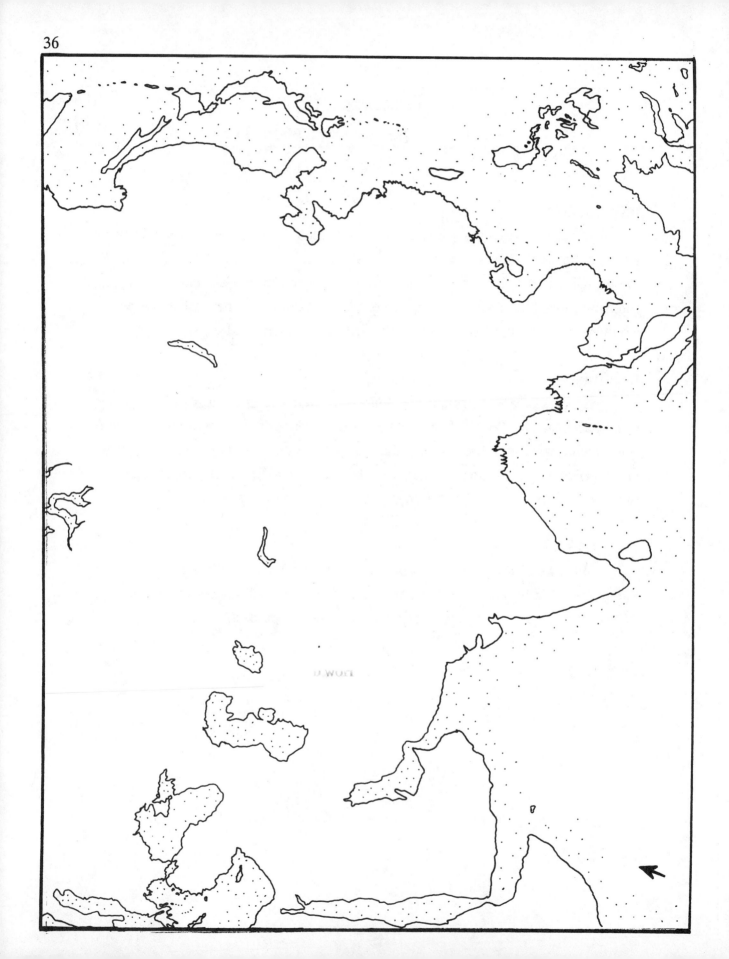

Exercise 18
Asia: European Influences in 1914

(Map 25.3)

Introduction

Asia, too, received the attentions of the Europeans. Some territories were acquired by the Europeans, others came strongly under the influence of the western powers. The United States also evinced an interest in the Pacific rim countries and claimed some territory for themselves. These western states felt themselves superior to the Asian and African people, and thus easily justified their imperialistic attitude by explaining that such oppression was of mutual benefit. Kipling's poem the "White Man's Burden" exemplifies this western feeling of superiority.

Locations

A. On the map provided identify the possessions or spheres of influence for the following western powers: The United States, Great Britain, Russia, Germany, the Dutch, Portugal

B. Also label the following regions of Asia: Persia, India, China, Korea, Philippines, Japan, Ceylon, East Indies

Questions

Compare and contrast British and Russian interests in Asia. What attracted each to the region? How did the Russians and British interact? With what results for the people of Asia? Which territories remained independent? How did they manage to remain so?

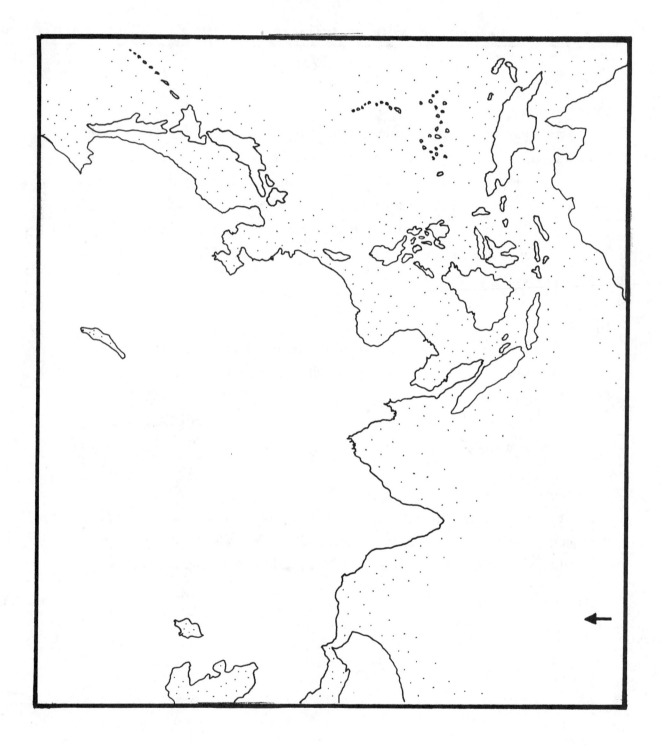

Exercise 19
China and Japan into the 20th Century

(Maps 25.1, 25.2, 25.3, 25.4)

Introduction

In about 1868 Japan's interest in the outside world increased dramatically. By 1875 Japan had gained control of several islands. Japan continued to extend her empire to the north, the south and to the mainland by means of a series of three wars.

In China, the 20th century has seen profound changes. Participation in the Long March defined a generation of Chinese. The Chinese today are the most populous nation on earth and the greatest communist power in the 1990's. This exercise traces the spheres of influence exerted over time by both the Chinese and Japanese.

Locations

A. First lightly shade in the areas of Russian, British and Japanese influences on the mainland and in the islands.

B. Next draw in the boundary of the Chinese Empire as of 1911, and the Chinese state as of ca. 1950.

C. Also locate and distinguish the following regions and cities on your map: Siam, Hong Kong, Taipei, Xinjing, Vladivostok, Macao, Taiwan, Philippines, Manchuria, Hunan, Canton, Beijing

D. Mark the following geographical features on your map: Altai Mountains, Sea of Japan, South China Sea, Pacific Ocean

Questions

Using map 24.4, list the areas acquired by Japan as of 1875 and as of 1914. What conflicts, if any, resulted from these acquisitions? What were the long term effects of these acquisitions?

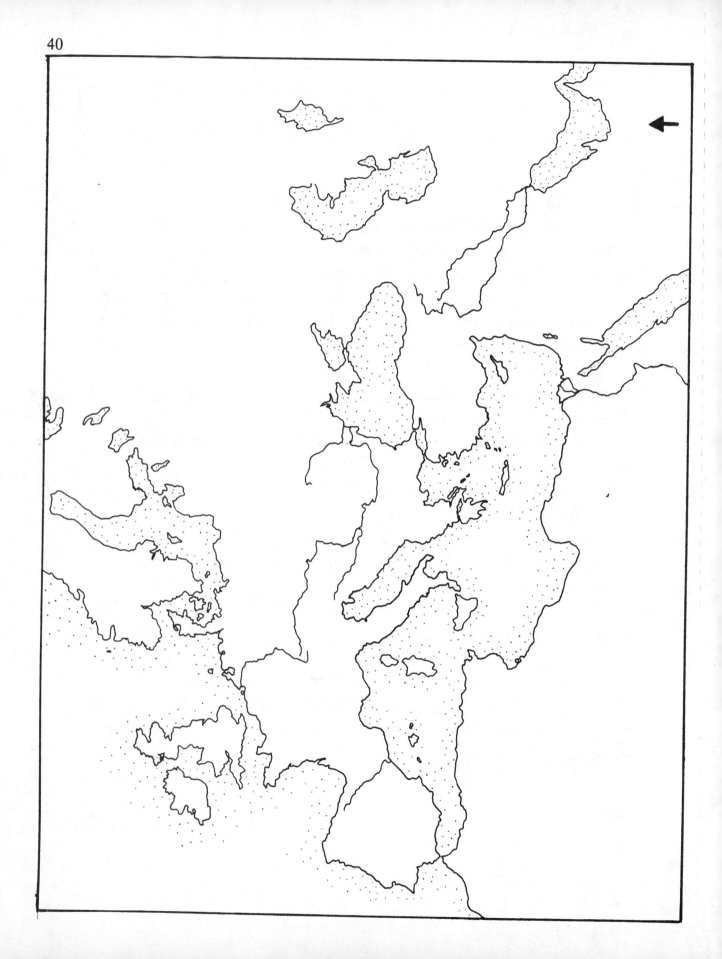

Exercise 20
Europe after World War I

(Maps 26.1, 26.3)

Introduction

World War I was one of the defining events of the twentieth century. The brutality, overwhelming magnitude, the length of the war, and its final settlement would prepare the road for yet another major conflict. Its destructiveness was a shock and disappointment to Europeans -- intellectual, industrial worker and farmer alike. Not surprisingly, the conflict was ignited by a confrontation between Austria and Serbia, after the heir to the Austrian throne was assassinated in Sarajevo, a Bosnian city.

This exercise compares the political divisions of Europe before and after the "Great War."

Locations

A. On the map provided use a dotted line to mark the boundaries of pre-World War I Europe. Mark the boundaries of the following states (do not label them yet): Spain, France, Belgium, Netherlands, Germany, Switzerland, Italy, Austria-Hungary, Serbia, Montenegro, Albania, Greece, Bulgaria, Rumania, Russia

B. Now with a solid line, mark the post World War I boundaries of, and label, the following states: France, Austria, Hungary, Germany, Yugoslavia, Czechoslovakia, Rumania, Bulgaria, Albania, Poland.

Questions

Where did Yugoslavia and Czechoslovakia come from? What happened to the territory of the Germans after the war? Who gained by Germany's losses? How did the Austro-Hungarian Empire fare in the new divisions of Europe? Finally, what result did this war have on European dominance of world affairs?

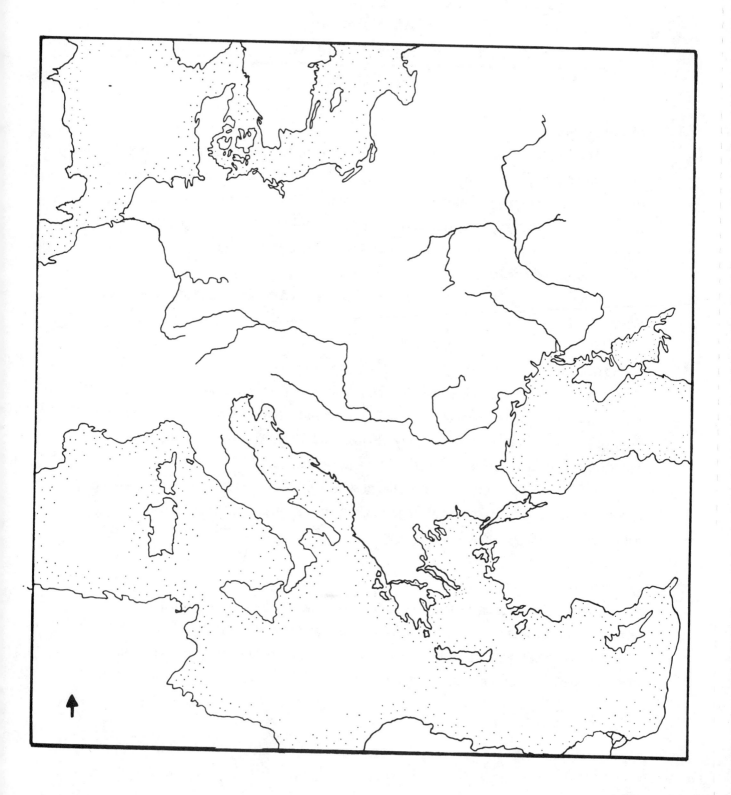

Exercise 21
Central Europe after World War II
(Maps 27.3, 28.4)

Introduction

In 1919 the people of Europe was optimistic, though in economic trouble. Then the infamous Great Depression hit, and would affect Americans and Europeans alike. The Germans were very hard hit by these financial setbacks and came to resent their position in the post war world. According to Heinrich Hauser (see text chapter 27) "An almost unbroken chain of homeless men extends the whole length of the great Hamburg-Berlin highway..." Only twenty years would pass before the next major conflagration would occur.

The economic disaster precipitated non-democratic political solutions to economic problems and the creation of authoritarian and totalitarian states. World War II was inevitable when one such power, the Nazi's, took hold in Germany and convinced the German people that, among other things, they needed and deserved more living space (*lebensraum*). Once again a massively destructive war was fought on European soil, with devastating demographic, material and psychological results. Here we will look at one result: the territorial settlement of Central Europe (where the greatest changes occurred) following the war.

Locations

A. On the map provided, label and draw in the 1949 boundaries of Germany, Poland, Czechoslovakia, Hungary Estonia, Latvia, Lithuania, Yugoslavia, Finland, Greece and France. Using different colored pencils lightly shade in the U.S., French, British and Soviet zones in Germany. Also shade in all the territory gained by the Soviet Union. Mark with a dotted line the "Iron Curtain" that went up after 1955.

B. Label or draw in the following geographical features: Black Sea, Danube River, Oder River, Baltic Sea and the Rhine River.

Questions

What were the general affects of this war on the population of Europe? Try to describe the "scene" in some detail. How long was Germany divided into Zones? Describe the division of Berlin. What territory was lost to Germany and to whom did it go? Territorially, who gained the most from the settlement after World War II?

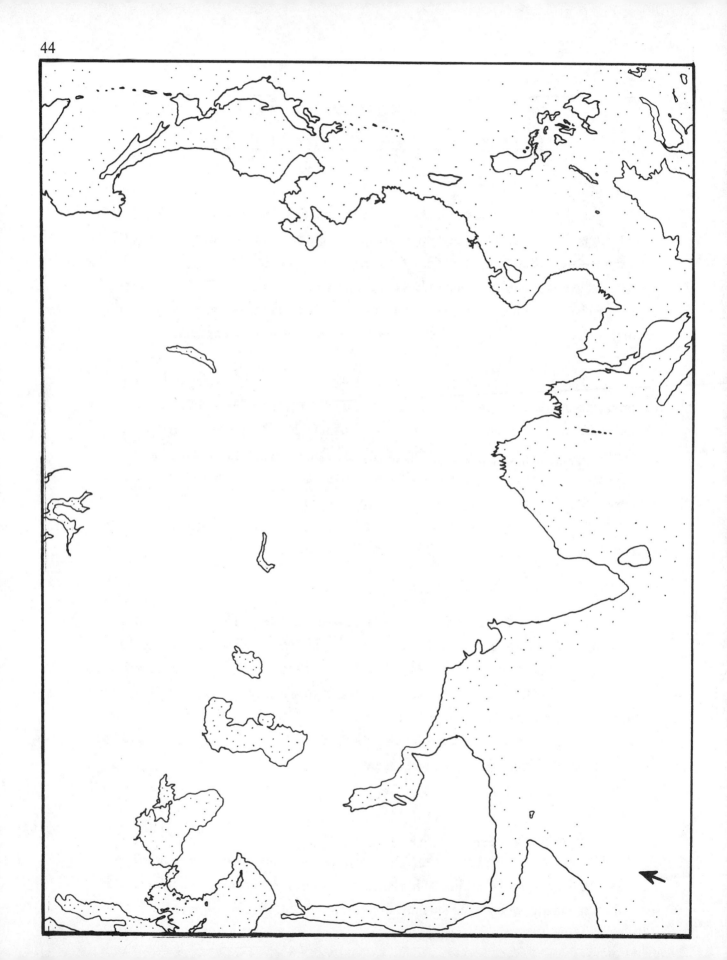

Exercise 22
The Middle East and Asia After World War II

(Maps 29.3, 29.4)

Introduction

World War II had a profound impact in the territories influenced and claimed by the European powers in Africa, Asia and the Middle East. Claims of independence and nationalistic anti-colony movements abounded. In Asia and the Middle East successful revolutionary attempts added up. India and Pakistan freed themselves from British rule. Other Asian countries also managed to loose the bonds of European control. In the Middle East, the growing nationalism of the Arabs helped put an end to colonial control, but they could not prevent the creation of a new Jewish state, Israel.

Locations

On the map provided draw the boundaries, label and provide the date of independence for the following states of the Middle East and Asia: Pakistan, India, Bangladesh, Burma, Laos, Vietnam, Cambodia, Philippines, Israel, Lebanon, Syria, Kuwait and Jordan

Questions

At the end of World War II a new conflict arose between the two major "super-powers," the erstwhile allies, the United States and Soviet Union. Briefly describe the nature of this conflict prior to 1980. What effect did their relations have on the politics of the Middle East? What specific factors generally encouraged the collapse of the European colonies?

Exercise 23

The Far East and Asia in the Later 20th Century

(Maps 30.1, 30.2, 31.1, 31.2, 32.1)

Introduction

Our world of the 20th century continues to transform itself. This exercise introduces you to the countries of Asia after World War II, revolutions, the Korean and Vietnam conflicts. These conflicts spurred the creation of new boundaries -- boundaries that are no more set in stone now than they had been in the centuries preceding ours.

Locations

A. On the map provided draw the boundaries and label the following states of the Far East: North Korea, South Korea, The People's Republic of China, Tibet, Japan, Russia, Taiwan (Republic of China), Mongolia, Bangladesh, India, Pakistan, Vietnam, Cambodia, Thailand, Laos, Philippines

B. Locate and label the following major cities: Lhasa, Seoul, Kwangju, New Delhi, Bombay, Tokyo, Kyoto, Hiroshima, Nagasaki, Manila, Hong Kong, Bangkok, Rangoon,

Questions

How has communism helped shape the states of Asia? What factors in the cultures of the Asian people contributed to their attraction to communism? What problems did the communist system solve? In what ways has it been successful in its goals? Unsuccessful?

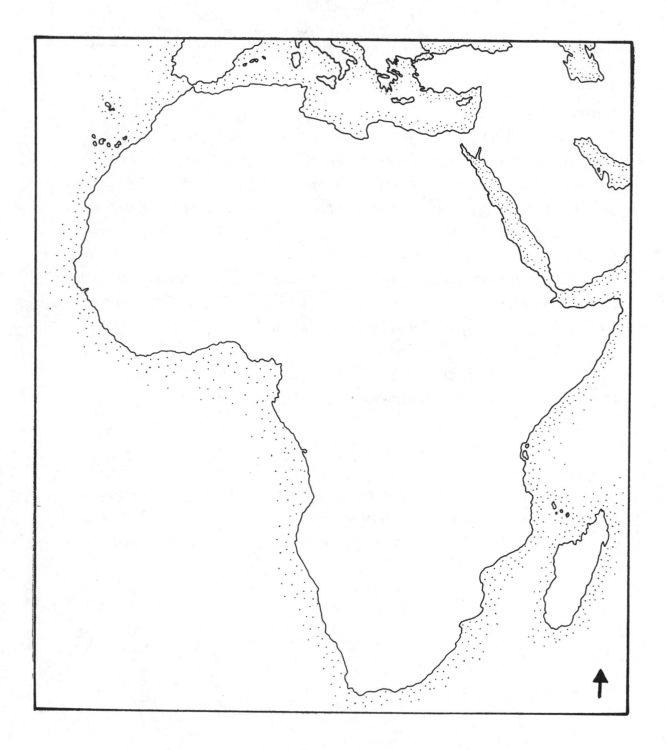

Exercise 24
Africa, the Near East and the Mediterranean After World War II

(Maps 33.1, 33.2, 33.3)

Introduction

Like other regions of the world, the countries of Africa and the Near East have spent the better part of the 20th century freeing themselves from the colonial and imperial powers. The boundaries of the African countries reflect colonial territories rather than "natural" cultural or economic regions. This fact has increased conflict and hindered the ability of some African states to rule and support themselves successfully and peacefully.

The states of the Arabian peninsula have proved more fortunate economically, due to their abundant and necessary resources (oil). This exercise introduces you to modern Africa and the Near East.

Locations

A. Africa -- draw in the boundaries of the following states: Morocco, Algeria, Libya, Egypt, Sudan, Ethiopia, Tanzania, Mozambique, Republic of South Africa, Namibia, Angola, Nigeria, Ghana, Ivory Coast and Liberia

B. Arabia --
draw in the boundaries of the following states: Saudi Arabia, Jordan, Kuwait, Bahrain, Yemen, South Yemen Oman. Next, shade in the major oil producing areas.

C. Also label the Mediterranean Sea, Persian Gulf, Red Sea, Italy, Cyprus, Greece, Turkey, Iraq, and Israel

Questions

What are the economic problems facing many of the Saharan and sub-Saharan African countries? What are the differences in the resources found in the east, west and southern tip of Africa? What have been the long term results of this uneven distribution of natural resources?

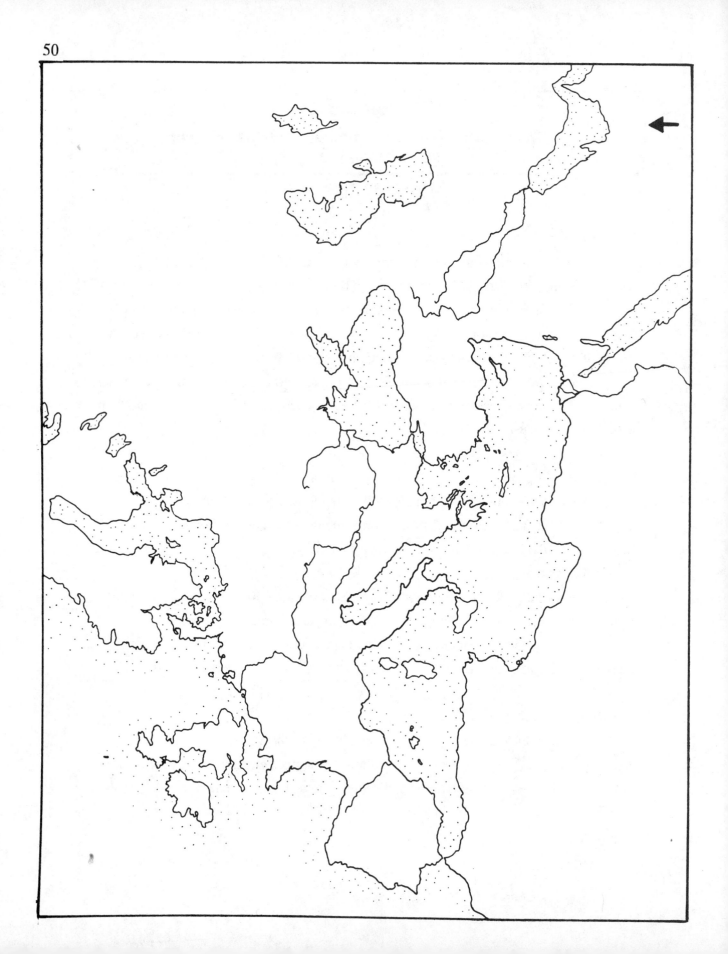

Exercise 25

The Future: Political and Cultural Boundaries in Europe

Introduction

You have seen the boundaries of the European world change continually over time. This is an exercise of your imagination. On the map provided draw the boundaries of Europe as you believe they will be fifty years from today. Mark on your map major changes in population that you predict (do you think large numbers, for example, of ethnic Albanians will move to another country or countries?). Do you believe there will be any more major wars on the order of the first and second world wars? Why or why not?

Next justify your predictions. Why do you believe the changes you suggest will occur? Use both current and past events to support your position.

Exercise 26
The Future: Political and Cultural Boundaries in Asia

Introduction

You have also seen the boundaries of the Asian world change continually over time. This is an exercise of your imagination. On the map provided draw the boundaries of Asia as you believe they will be fifty years from today. Mark on your map major changes in population that you predict. (Do you think, for example, that population control measures in India will be successful?) Do you believe there will be any more major wars on the order of the first and second world wars? Why or why not?

Next justify your predictions. Why do you believe the changes you suggest will occur? Use both current and past events to support your position.

EXTRA MAPS

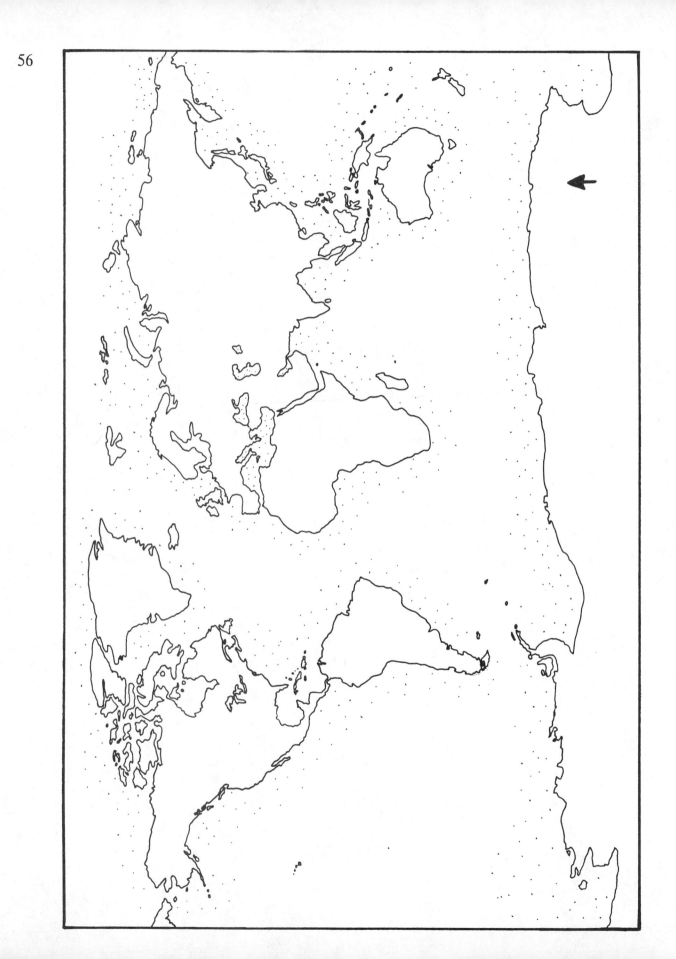

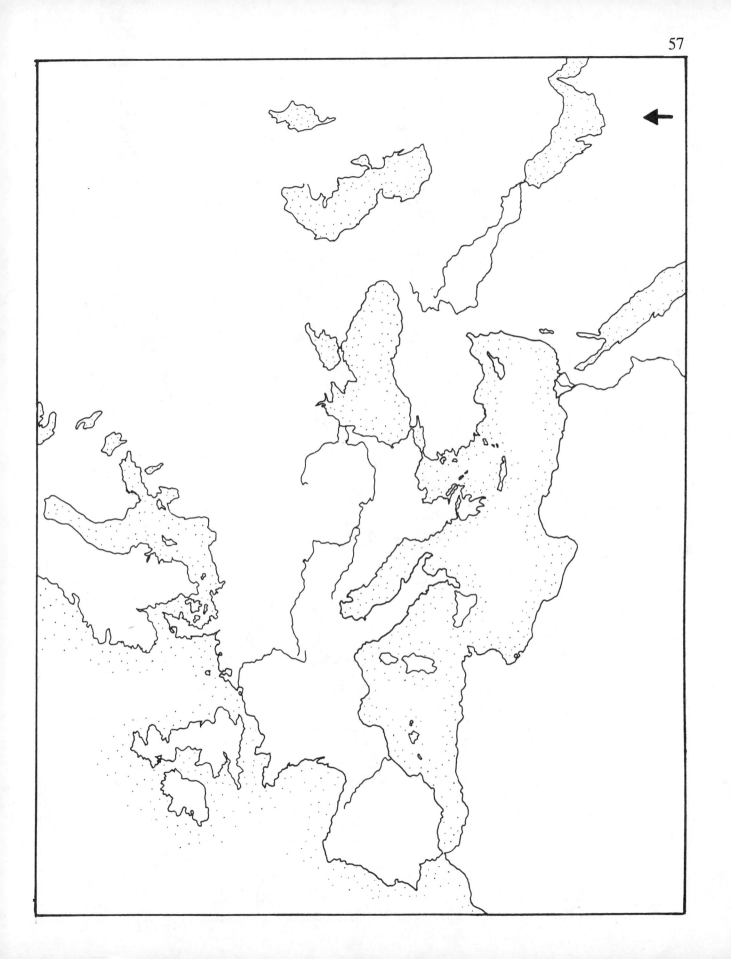

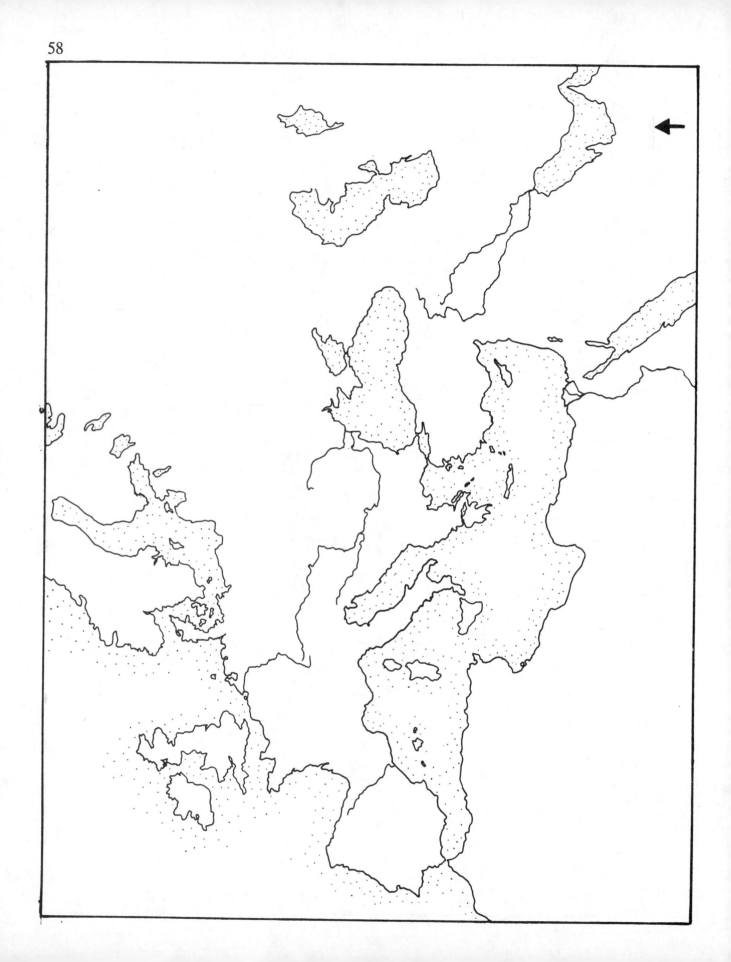

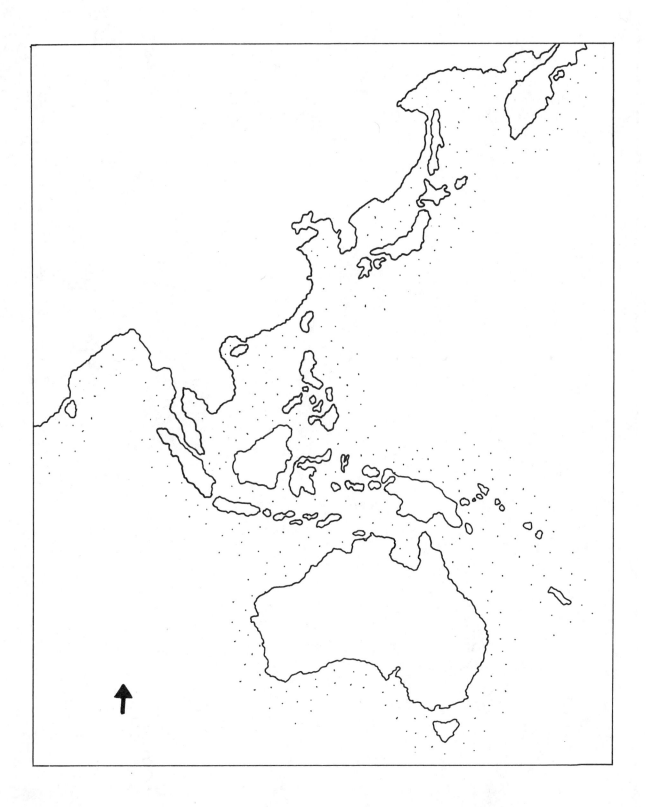

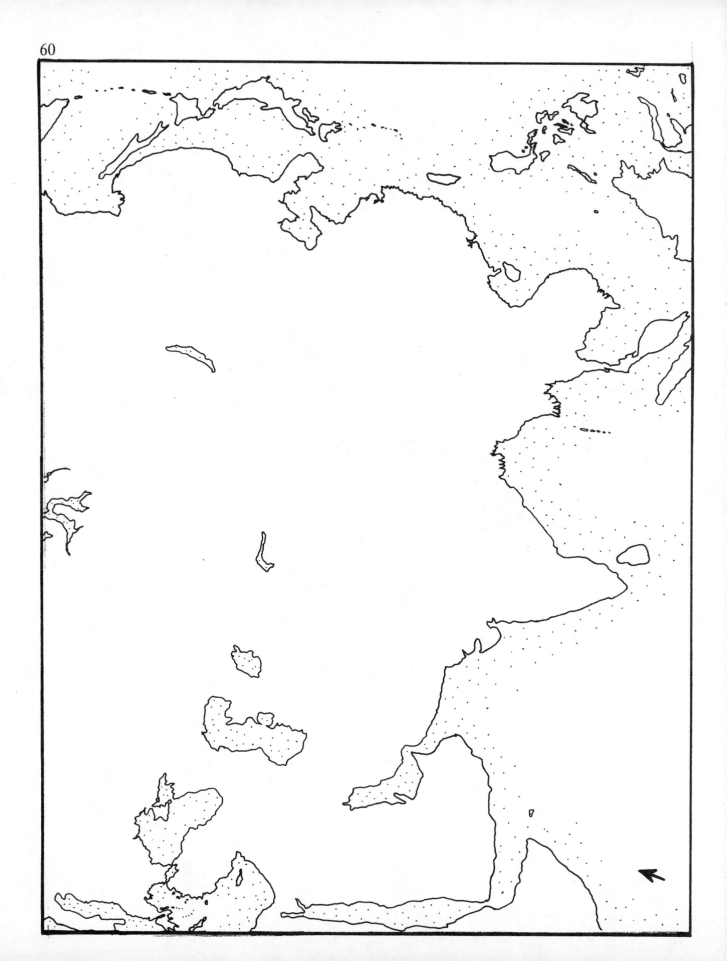

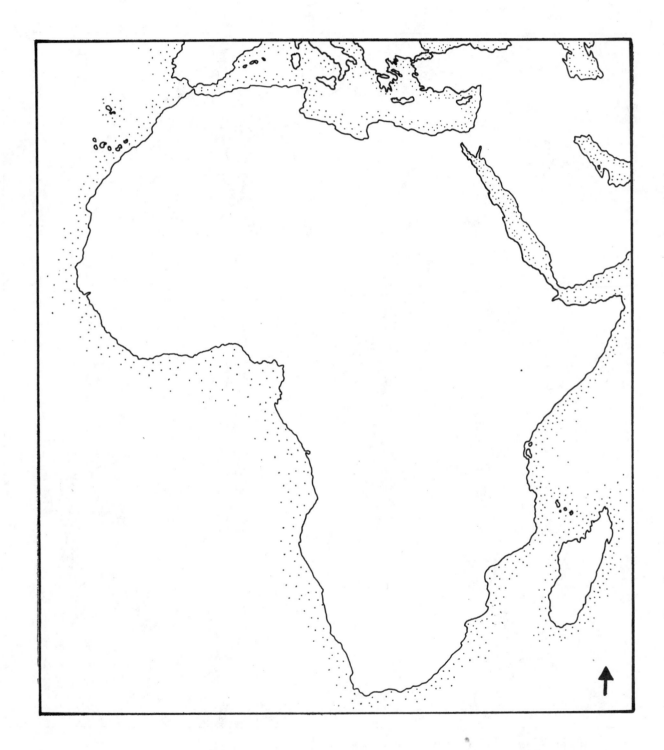